AF088398

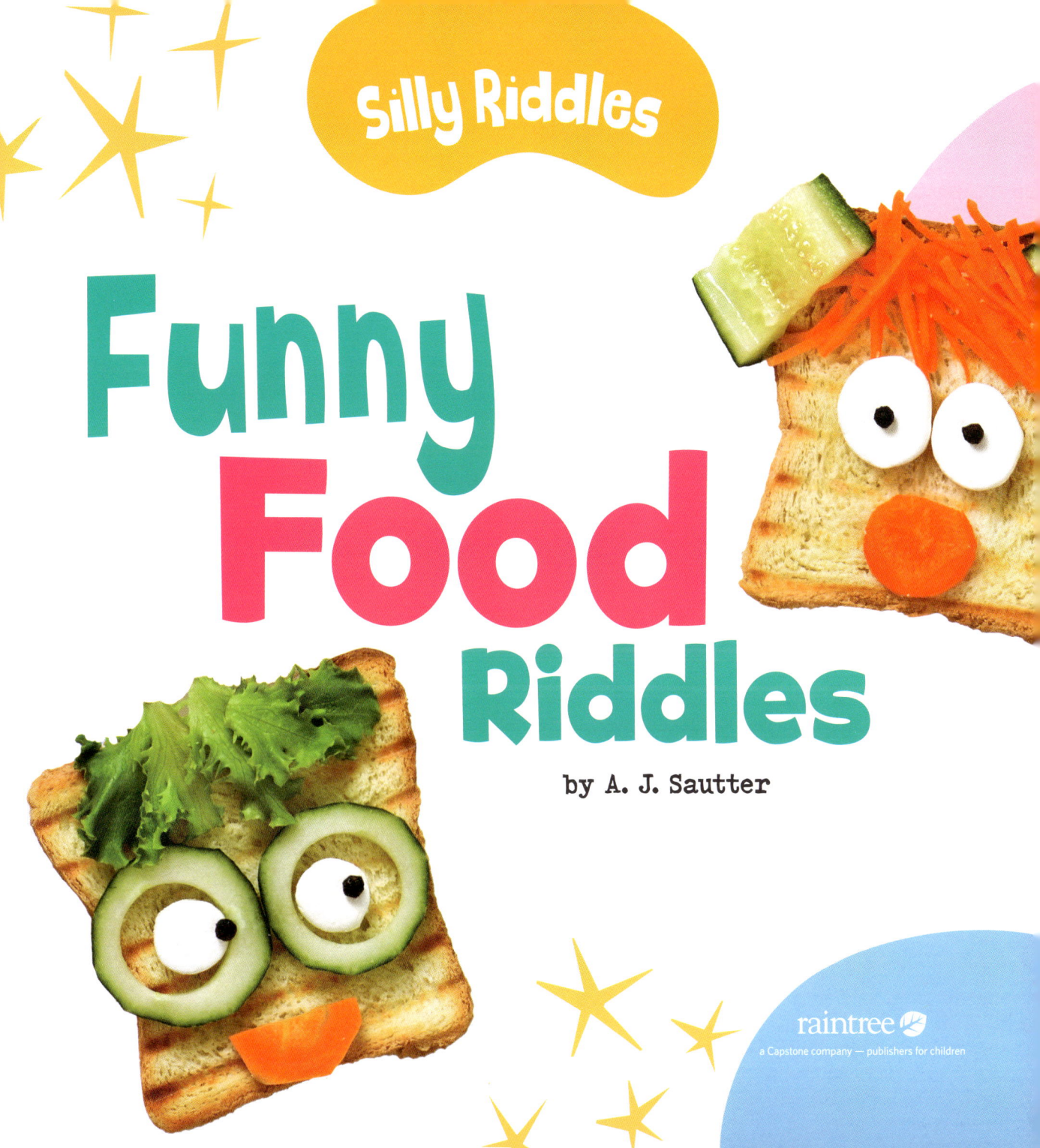

Raintree is an imprint of Capstone Global Library Limited, a company incorporated in England and Wales having its registered office at 264 Banbury Road, Oxford, OX2 7DY – Registered company number: 6695582

www.raintree.co.uk
myorders@raintree.co.uk

Hardback edition text © Capstone Global Library Limited 2024
Paperback edition text © Capstone Global Library Limited 2025

The moral rights of the proprietor have been asserted. All rights reserved. No part of this publication may be reproduced in any form or by any means (including photocopying or storing it in any medium by electronic means and whether or not transiently or incidentally to some other use of this publication) without the written permission of the copyright owner, except in accordance with the provisions of the Copyright, Designs and Patents Act 1988 or under the terms of a licence issued by the Copyright Licensing Agency, 5th Floor, Shackleton House, 4 Battle Bridge Lane, London, SE1 2HX (www.cla.co.uk). Applications for the copyright owner's written permission should be addressed to the publisher.

ISBN 978 1 3982 5411 4 (hardback)
ISBN 978 1 3982 5412 1 (paperback)

Editorial Credits
Editor: Aaron Sautter; Designer: Jaime Willems; Media Researcher: Rebekah Hubstenberger; Production Specialist: Whitney Schaefer

Photo Credits
Getty Images: Isabelle Rozenbaum, 7 (cherries); Shutterstock: Aleksandrs Samuilovs, 17 (toast), Bauwimauwi, 8 (apple, oranges), bonchan, 15, Bored Photography, 9 (grapes), Chiyacat, 19, colnihko, design element (colour eye), D_M, cover (mushrooms), Elena. D, 21 (sandwiches), Fascinadora, 17 (nuts), Freer, 12 (potato), GSDesign, 5 (apples), Iurii Stepanov, 12 (onion), JIANG HONGYAN, 7 (pears), M. Unal Ozmen, 20 (ice cream), Maks Narodenko, 10, MaraZe, cover (watermelon), 6, 18 (soup), NATALIA61, design element (googly eye), Nataliia Pyzhova, 20 (doughnut), New Africa, 4 (strawberries), 13 (corn), oksana2010, design element (paper cutouts), 14, Perfectorius, design element (symbols), photomaster, 18 (turkey), Stephen Mcsweeny, 8 (banana split), StockArtRoom, design element (shapes), Tanarch, 11, Tanya Sid, 5 (blueberries), VladyslaV Travel photo, 16, zefirchik06, cover (toast)

British Library Cataloguing in Publication Data
A full catalogue record for this book is available from the British Library.

Printed and bound in India.

Contents

Fruity fun 4

Puzzling produce 10

Mind-bending munchies 16

Glossary 22

Find out more 23

Index 24

About the author 24

Words in **bold** are in the glossary.

Fruity fun

1. I am sweet and fruity. Part of my name can be used to sip drinks. What am I?

Answers!

1. A strawberry

2. What fruit always feels sad and **depressed**?

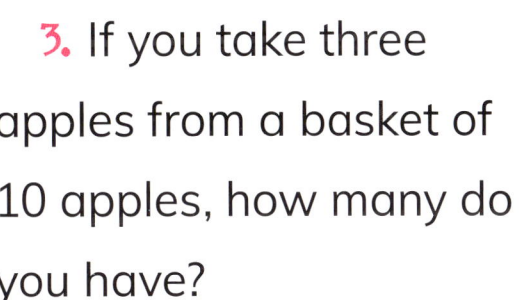

3. If you take three apples from a basket of 10 apples, how many do you have?

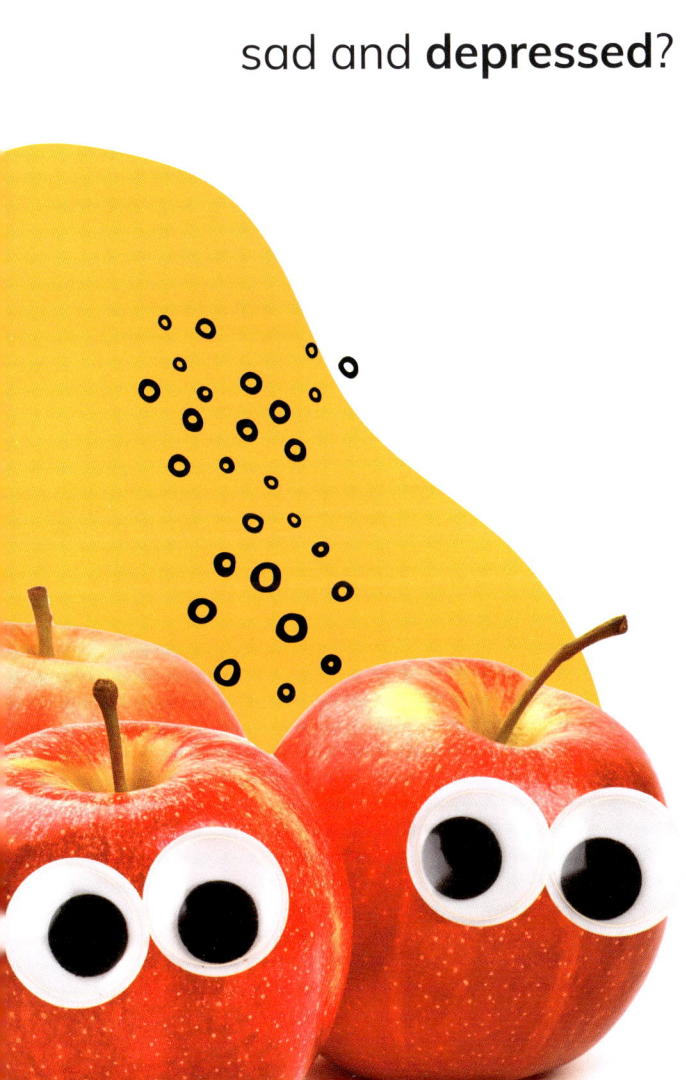

Answers!

2. Blueberries.
3. Three apples. You took three of them.

4. When should you go at red and stop at green?

5. A farmer sells his melons at the market. He sells half of them, including half a melon. There is one whole melon left. How many melons did he take to market?

Answers!

4. When you're eating watermelon.
5. Three melons.

6. I wear a red coat and there's a stone in my throat. What am I?

7. What fruit is never found alone?

Answers!

6. A cherry.
7. A pear.

8. How do you pronounce banana split?

Answers!

8. Ban-ana.

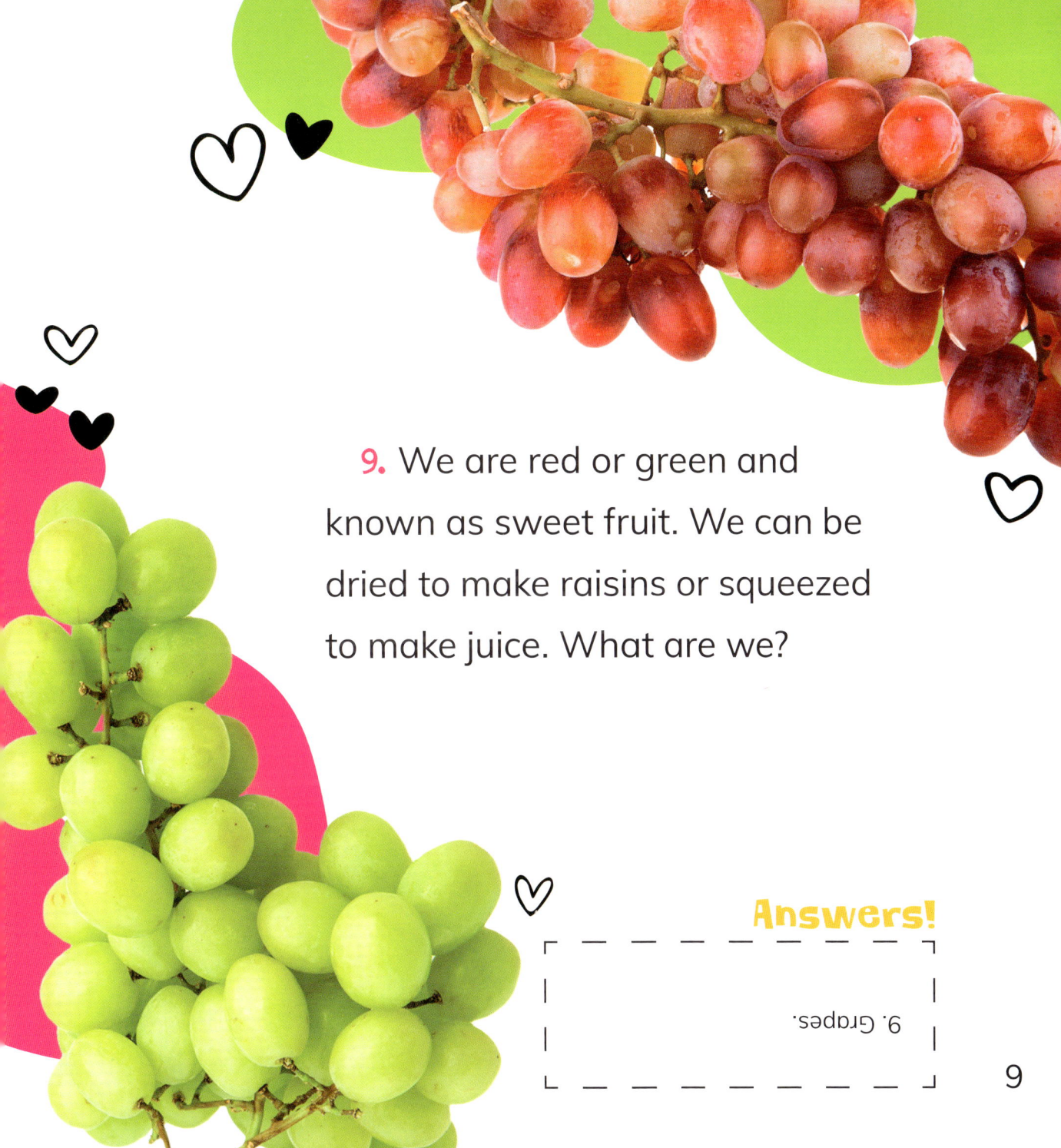

9. We are red or green and known as sweet fruit. We can be dried to make raisins or squeezed to make juice. What are we?

Answers!

9. Grapes.

Puzzling produce

10. What is bright orange, green on top and sounds like a parrot?

Answers!

10. A carrot.

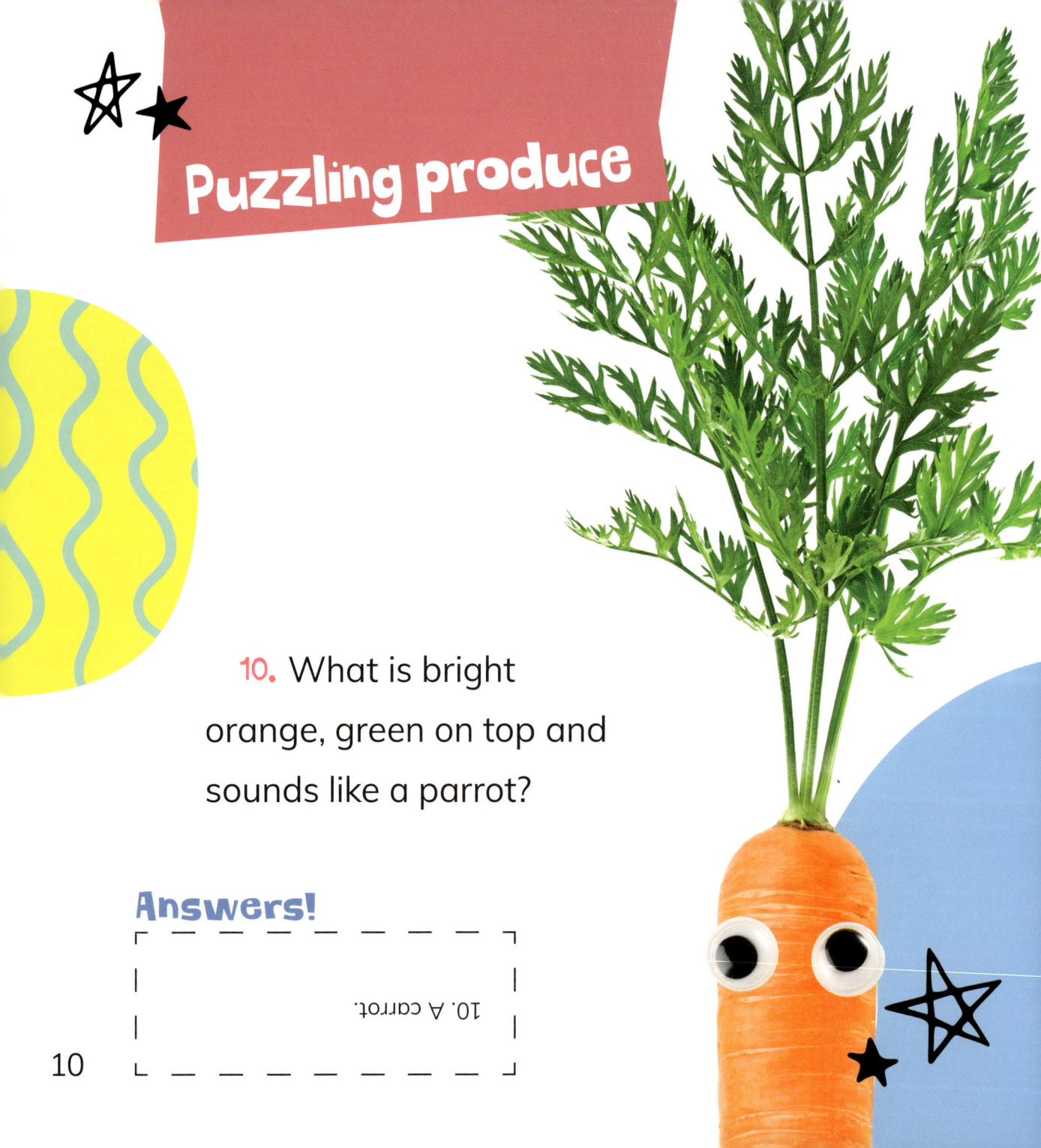

11. What food is the most fun to hang out with?

12. What award do you win for eating your vegetables?

Answers!

11. A mushroom, because he's a **fungi!**

12. The Nobel Peas Prize!

13. When you cut me open, you start to cry. What am I?

14. What has many eyes, but cannot see?

Answers!

13. An onion.
14. A potato.

15. Why should you never tell a secret in a corn field?

16. How do you spell aubergine backwards?

Answers!

15. Because there are so many ears.
16. A-U-B-E-R-G-I-N-E B-A-C-K-W-A-R-D-S.

17. What should you do if there's vegetable soup on the **menu**?

18. What kind of table can people eat?

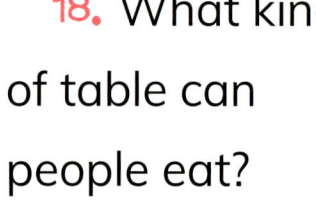

17. Wipe it off.
18. A veggie-table!

19. What is the cleverest vegetable?

20. What type of veggies do sailors hate?

Answers!

19. Human beans.
20. Leeks.

Mind-bending munchies

21. If you can get a dozen eggs for 12 pence, how many can you get for 1 pound?

Answers!

21. 100. Each egg costs a penny.

22. What does a slice of toast wear to bed?

23. What is a robot's favourite snack?

Answers!

22. Its jam-mies!
23. Mixed nuts.

24. Why can you never take a turkey out for dinner?

25. What is the easiest way to make soup taste terrible?

Answers!

24. Because it just gobble, gobble, gobbles its food!

25. Change the U to an A. Then "soup" becomes "soap".

26. What did Pastarella dream about doing?

27. It has no **hinges**, no lock and no lid. Yet within it golden treasure is hid. What is it?

Answers!

26. Going to the meat ball.
27. An egg.

28. What kind of nut has a hole in the middle?

29. What is the loudest of all desserts?

Answers!

28. A doughnut.
29. Ice-scream.

30. What is the scariest food to eat?

Answers!

30. A sand-witch!

Glossary

aubergine a plant that grows dark purple vegetables

depressed to feel sad and gloomy

fungi organisms that have no leaves, flowers or roots; mushrooms and moulds are types of fungi

hinge a device that lets a door, gate or lid swing back and forth

menu a list of food and drinks available at a restaurant

Find out more

Books

My Very Very Very Very Very Very Very Silly Book of Jokes, Matt Lucas (Egmont, 2020)

The Kids' Book of Awesome Riddles, Amanda Learmonth (Buster Books, 2019)

Websites

40+ Food Riddles for Every Chef
boxofpuns.com/food-riddles/

Food Jokes and Riddles for Kids
enchantedlearning.com/jokes/topics/food.shtml

Food Riddles and Brain Teasers
logiclike.com/en/food-riddles

Index

apples 5, 8

bananas 8
blueberries 5

carrots 10
cherries 7
corn 13

desserts 20

eggs 16, 19

grapes 9

melons 6
mushrooms 11

nuts 17, 20

onions 12
oranges 8

pasta 19
pears 7
potatoes 12

sandwiches 21
soup 14, 18
strawberries 4

toast 17
turkeys 18

vegetables 11, 14–15

About the author

A. J. Sautter is an author and editor of dozens of kids' books on everything from aliens to zombies. He enjoys reading, going to the cinema and going for long walks with his fluffy, adorable dogs.